ENJOY WITHOUT WITHOUT SOY

Easy and Delicious Soy-Free Recipes for Kids With Allergies

by KATRINA JORGENSEN

CONSULTANT
Amy Durkan MS, RDN, CDN
Nutrition Research Manager
Mount Sinai Medical Center
New York, NY

CAPSTONE PRESS
a capstone imprint

Edge Books are published by Capstone Press,
1710 Roe Crest Drive, North Mankato, Minnesota 56003
www.mycapstone.com

Library of Congress Cataloging-in-Publication Data
Cataloging-in-Publication data is on file with the Library of Congress.
ISBN 978-1-4914-8056-4 (library binding)
ISBN 978-1-4914-8061-8 (eBook PDF)

Editorial Credits
Anna Butzer, editor; Heidi Thompson, designer; Morgan Walters, media researcher;
Sarah Schuette, food stylist; Kathy McColley, production specialist

Design Elements
Shutterstock: avian, design element, Katerina Kirilova, design element, Lena Pan, design
element, Marco Govel, design element, mexrix, design element, Sabina Pittak, design
element, STILLFX, design element, swatchandsoda, design element

Photography by Capstone Studio: Karon Dubke

Editor's note:
Capstone cannot ensure that any food is allergen-free. The only way to be sure a food is
safe is to read all labels carefully, every time. Cross-contamination is also a risk for those
with food allergies. Please call food companies to make sure their manufacturing processes
avoid cross-contamination. Also, always be sure to clean hands, surfaces, and tools
before cooking.

Printed and bound in the USA.
009675F16

TABLE OF CONTENTS

WHAT IS A FOOD ALLERGY?

Our bodies are armed with immune systems. It's the immune system's job to fight infections, viruses, and invaders. Sometimes the immune system identifies a certain food as one of these invaders and attacks it. While our immune system fights, a chemical response is triggered and causes an allergic reaction. Reactions vary greatly from a mild skin irritation to having trouble breathing. Any time you feel you are having a reaction, tell an adult immediately.

The best way to avoid having an allergic reaction is to be aware of what you are eating. Be careful not to consume the allergen that affects you. If you are not sure if that allergen is in a food, ask an adult or read the ingredient label of the food container before eating. Unfortunately, allergens can sometimes be hard to identify in an ingredient list. Check out http://www.foodallergy.org for a full list of hidden soy terms.

Avoiding food allergens can be hard to manage, especially when they are found in so many of our favorite foods. This cookbook will take you on a culinary journey to explore many of the dishes you've had to avoid because of a soy allergy.

Kitchen Safety

A safe kitchen is a fun kitchen! Always start your recipes with clean hands, surfaces, and tools. Wash your hands and any tools you may use in future steps of a recipe, especially when handling raw meat. Make sure you have an adult nearby to help you with any task you don't feel comfortable doing, such as cutting vegetables or carrying hot pans.

ALLERGY ALERTS AND TIPS

Have other food allergies? No problem.
Check out the list at the end of each recipe
for substitutions for other common allergens.
Look out for other cool tips and ideas too!

CONVERSIONS

1/4 teaspoon	1.25 grams or milliliters
1/2 teaspoon	2.5 g or mL
1 teaspoon	5 g or mL
1 tablespoon	15 g or mL
1/4 cup	57 g (dry) or 60 mL (liquid)
1/3 cup	75 g (dry) or 80 mL (liquid)
1/2 cup	114 g (dry) or 125 mL (liquid)
2/3 cup	150 g (dry) or 160 mL (liquid)
3/4 cup	170 g (dry) or 175 mL (liquid)
1 cup	227 g (dry) or 240 mL (liquid)
1 quart	950 mL

Fahrenheit (°F)	Celsius (°C)
325°	160°
350°	180°
375°	190°
400°	200°
425°	220°
450°	230°

CHERRY PIE BREAKFAST BARS

Pie for breakfast? It may sound like an early morning dessert, but these bars can give you a nutritious start to your day. The dates and cherries provide a sweet flavor without adding sugar.

Prep Time: 2 hours 15 minutes
(2 hours inactive)

Makes 8 bars

Ingredients

½ cup pitted dates

2 tablespoons water

1 cup rolled oats

½ cup dried cherries

Tools

food processor

measuring cups/spoons

medium baking sheet

parchment paper

chef's knife

1. Combine the dates and water in a food processor. Pulse until the mixture is mostly smooth.

2. Add the rolled oats. Then turn food processor on high for about 30 seconds.

3. Put the cherries in the food processor bowl and pulse about 10 times. The cherries should be chunky.

4. Line the baking sheet with parchment paper. Press the dough mixture into the pan with your hands, making sure it is spread out evenly.

5. Place in freezer for two hours to set.

6. Remove from freezer and allow to thaw slightly, about 15 minutes. Slice into eight bars.

7. Store leftovers in refrigerator in an airtight container for up to two weeks.

CHEF'S TIP

Does cherry pie make you squirm?
Any dried fruits can be used.
Try apples, apricots, pineapple,
or even mango instead!

HOMEMADE TOASTER PASTRIES

You can have a fruit-filled blast by making toaster pastries from scratch, and you don't even need a toaster! Packaged breakfast foods at the grocery store might have soy, but these tasty pastries are soy free.

Prep Time: 30 minutes

Cook Time: 30 minutes

Makes 8 pastries

Ingredients

2 cups all-purpose flour, plus a little
   more for rolling out the dough

1 tablespoon sugar

½ teaspoon salt

⅔ cup shortening

¼ cup cold water

¼ cup your favorite jam

Icing

1 cup powdered sugar

2 tablespoons rice milk

1 teaspoon vanilla extract

Tools

large baking sheet

parchment paper

large mixing bowl

measuring spoons/cups

fork

rolling pin

pizza cutter

spatula

small mixing bowl

Allergen Alert!

If you need to avoid wheat, use
wheat-free flour mix instead.

1. Preheat oven to 350°F. Line a baking sheet with parchment paper and set aside.

2. In a mixing bowl, combine the flour, sugar, and salt. Using a fork, mix in the shortening until it becomes crumbly, like wet sand.

3. Add water and mix gently with fingers until a dough ball forms. Add water if it's too dry.

4. Sprinkle a couple tablespoons of flour on a clean surface and place the dough ball on it. Use the rolling pin to flatten the ball into a rectangle about ⅛ inch (0.3 centimeter) thick.

5. Cut 16, 3 x 5-inch (7.6 x 12.7-cm) rectangles using the pizza cutter. Space evenly on the baking sheet about 1 inch (2.5 cm) apart.

6. Spread 1 tablespoon of jam on eight of the dough rectangles, leaving about ¼ inch (0.6 cm) of space from the edges.

7. Place the plain dough rectangles over the jam-filled rectangles. Press the tines of the fork around the edges to seal.

8. Using the fork, poke a few holes in the top of each pastry. Then place the baking sheet in the oven for about 20 minutes, or until the pastries are golden brown. Allow to cool for 10 minutes before icing.

9. Combine all icing ingredients in a mixing bowl. Stir well with a fork until smooth.

10. Ice the pastries by dipping a fork into the icing bowl and drizzling it over the pastries.

11. Store leftovers in the freezer for up to one month. To reheat, place in oven at 350°F for about five minutes.

APPLE PUFF

CEREAL

Start off your day with a bowl of apple cinnamon delight! These sweet puffs have a crunchy outside and a light, airy inside. Unlike many cereals from the grocery store, this recipe will keep soy away from the breakfast table.

Prep Time: 15 minutes

Cook Time: 15 minutes

Makes 2 cups cereal

Ingredients

1 cup flour

¼ teaspoon salt

1 teaspoon vanilla extract

½ teaspoon honey

½ teaspoon ground cinnamon

2 tablespoons applesauce

½ tablespoon olive oil

Tools

large baking sheet

parchment paper

food processor

measuring cups/spoons

spatula

1. Preheat oven to 350°F. Line a baking sheet with parchment paper and set aside.

2. In a food processor set on high, combine all ingredients until a dough forms.

3. Remove the dough from the food processor with a spatula. Using clean hands, roll the dough into small balls, about the size of a grape.

4. Place the puffs about 1 inch (2.5 cm) apart on the baking sheet.

5. Put the baking sheet in the oven and bake for about seven minutes. Take out the baking sheet and swirl the pan around to roll the puffs over. Return pan to oven to finish baking for an additional eight minutes.

6. Remove from the oven and allow to cool completely before placing in an airtight container.

7. Serve with your favorite milk for breakfast or a snack!

CHEF'S TIP

Don't just eat this with milk for breakfast! Make a parfait with layers of creamy yogurt, fresh fruit, and crunchy apple puffs!

CHICKEN POT PIE SOUP

Indulge in all the flavors of chicken pot pie, but without the soy! Juicy chicken and tender vegetables combine to tantalize your taste buds in this creamy recipe. Warm up the burners for a hearty soup that will fill you up!

Prep Time: 15 minutes

Cook Time: 30 minutes

Serves 4

Ingredients

2 chicken breasts

1 tablespoon oil, such as olive oil

1 small onion

1 stalk celery

1 tablespoon butter

2 tablespoons all-purpose flour

4 cups chicken broth

1 cup milk

1 16-ounce package frozen vegetable mix

1 teaspoon salt

½ teaspoon ground black pepper

Tools

cutting board

chef's knife

measuring cups/spoons

skillet

tongs

large soup pot

spoon

Allergen Alert!

Milk and butter are a no-go if you're avoiding dairy, but no worries! Just use coconut or rice milk instead of regular milk. Soy-free, nondairy butter will work instead of butter.

If you cannot eat wheat, use rice flour instead of all-purpose flour.

Make sure you check the label of your chicken broth to be sure it is soy-free!

1. Cut the chicken breasts into 1-inch (2.5-cm) cubes on the cutting board with the chef's knife.

2. Heat the oil in a skillet on a burner set on medium-high. Add the chicken and use the tongs to flip and stir. Cook about five minutes, or until no longer pink inside. Remove from heat and set aside.

3. Clean your knife and cutting board. Then chop the onion and celery into small pieces and set aside.

4. Add the butter to the large soup pot and melt over medium heat.

5. Put the onion and celery in the pot and stir gently. Allow to cook for about three to four minutes, or until the vegetables begin to soften.

6. Sprinkle the flour over the vegetables and stir until absorbed into the butter.

7. Pour in the chicken broth and milk, and stir quickly.

8. Increase the heat to medium-high until the soup begins to bubble softly. Reduce the heat to medium.

9. Add the frozen vegetables, salt, pepper, and the cooked chicken to the pot.

10. Cook for 30 minutes before serving.

CHICKEN CRANBERRY SALAD
LETTUCE WRAPS

Crispy lettuce makes the perfect package for delicious ingredients in these tasty wraps! Mix in a tangy homemade sauce to go with your scrumptious meal.

Prep Time: 15 minutes

Cook Time: 5 minutes

Makes 4 wraps

Ingredients

1 head Boston lettuce

1 chicken breast

1 tablespoon olive oil

1 Granny Smith apple

1 celery stalk

¾ cup olive oil mayonnaise

½ teaspoon honey

½ teaspoon Dijon mustard

½ cup dried cranberries

1 teaspoon salt

Tools

paper towels

cutting board

chef's knife

skillet

measuring cups/spoons

tongs

mixing bowl

spoon

1. Carefully pull off about 8 leaves of lettuce. Rinse well and place on paper towels to dry. Set aside.

2. Cut the chicken breast into 1-inch (2.5-cm) cubes. Add the oil to the skillet and heat over a burner set to medium.

3. Add the chicken and turn the pieces with tongs. Cook until no longer pink inside. When the chicken is done, set aside in the skillet to cool almost completely.

4. Clean your cutting board and knife. Then chop the apple into ½-inch (1.3-cm) cubes and discard the core.

5. Chop the celery into ½-inch (1.3-cm) pieces.

6. Add the apple, celery, mayonnaise, honey, mustard, cranberries, and salt to a mixing bowl. Stir to combine.

7. When the chicken is cooled, add it to the mixing bowl and toss lightly until coated.

8. To assemble the wraps, stack two lettuce leaves on top of each other. Spoon about ½ cup of the chicken salad in the center. Fold the sides in and roll at the same time to envelop the filling.

9. Serve cold, and store leftovers in the refrigerator for up to three days.

CHEF'S TIP

Try using mango, pineapple, or grapes instead of apple. Raisins, dates, or dried apricots can be used instead of dried cranberries.

GREEK TURKEY BURGERS

WITH CUCUMBER TZATZIKI

Forget the traditional burger!
Go Greek by adding a cool and
refreshing cucumber tzatziki sauce
to a traditional turkey burger.

Prep Time: 15 minutes

Cook Time: 15 minutes

Makes 4 burgers

Ingredients

Cucumber Tzatziki

½ English cucumber

1 clove garlic

¼ cup coconut cream

1 teaspoon lemon juice

¼ teaspoon salt

⅛ teaspoon ground black pepper

Turkey Burgers

2 cloves garlic

¼ cup fresh oregano

1 lemon

1 teaspoon salt

½ teaspoon ground black pepper

1 ½ pounds (24 ounces) ground turkey

1 tablespoon olive oil

4 slices pita bread

Tools

cutting board

chef's knife

grater

2 mixing bowls

measuring cups/spoons

micro-grater

skillet

spatula

Allergen Alert!

Read the pita bread label carefully to make sure it is certified soy-free.

If you are avoiding wheat, make sure you choose a variety that uses an alternative type of flour too.

1. For the tzatziki, cut the cucumber in half lengthwise. Then scoop out the seeds with a spoon. Grate half of the cucumber and place in a mixing bowl. Set aside the other half.

2. Chop the garlic finely and place in a mixing bowl. Add the coconut cream, lemon juice, salt, and pepper to the mixing bowl. Stir to combine and store in refrigerator until ready to use.

3. For the burgers, chop the garlic finely and toss in a mixing bowl.

4. Pull the leaves off of the fresh oregano and chop lightly. Add to bowl.

5. Zest the yellow part of the lemon peel using the micro-grater over the mixing bowl.

6. Add the salt, ground pepper, and ground turkey to the bowl. Mix gently with your hands until all ingredients are evenly mixed.

7. Divide the meat into 4 evenly-shaped balls. Flatten into round patties.

8. Heat the oil in the skillet over medium heat. Carefully place the patties in the hot oil, avoiding splatters.

9. Cook about six minutes on each side, or until no longer pink inside. Use the spatula for flipping.

10. To assemble the burgers, open the pita bread and slide a burger in. Then place 2 tablespoons of the tzatziki on top of each burger.

11. Serve immediately.

SESAME BEEF SKEWERS

Typical Asian cuisine uses soy as a key ingredient. But you can still enjoy a similar soy flavor with coconut aminos! Give your beef skewers a zingy Asian flare with this easy recipe.

Prep Time: 1 hour 15 minutes
(1 hour inactive)

Cook Time: 4 minutes

Makes 12 skewers

Ingredients

1 pound (16 oz) flank steak

2 cloves garlic

2 green onions

1-inch piece of fresh ginger

¼ cup coconut aminos

2 tablespoons chili-garlic sauce

2 tablespoons toasted sesame oil

1 tablespoon rice wine vinegar

cooking spray

Tools

cutting board

chef's knife

mixing bowl

micro-grater

measuring cups/spoons

whisk

gallon-size zip-top bag

12 wooden skewers

baking sheet

aluminum foil

Allergens Eradicated!

No major food allergens found here!

1. Using the cutting board and chef's knife, cut the flank steak into long, ½-inch (1.3-cm) thick strips. Set aside.

2. Clean your cutting board and knife. Then chop the garlic and green onions into very small pieces and set aside.

3. Using the micro-grater, carefully grate the ginger over a cutting board. Add it to the mixing bowl, along with the garlic and onions.

4. Add the coconut aminos, chili-garlic sauce, sesame oil, and vinegar to the mixing bowl. Whisk until mixed.

5. Place the marinade and beef into a zip-top bag. Using fingers, squish the beef until coated. Place the bag in the refrigerator for one hour.

6. Soak skewers in water while meat marinates.

7. Place the oven rack 4 to 6 inches (10 to 15 cm) below the broiler. Set the broiler on high. Line a baking sheet with aluminum foil. Place a wire cooling rack on top of the aluminum foil and spray with cooking spray.

8. Thread the skewers through the slices of meat. Discard the leftover marinade.

9. Place the skewers on the wire cooling rack. Then set the baking sheet in the oven.

10. Use tongs to turn over the skewers after two minutes. Cook an additional two minutes.

11. Remove from the oven and allow to cool for five minutes before serving hot.

ASIAN  NOODLES

Looking for a quick and easy Eastern-inspired dish to complement your meal? Savory noodles and crunchy vegetables provide flavor without soy!

Prep Time: 15 minutes

Cook Time: 10 minutes

Serves 4

Ingredients

8 ounces rice noodles

2 cloves garlic

1 small onion

2 tablespoons oil, such as olive oil

1 10-ounce bag broccoli slaw

½ cup coconut aminos

1 teaspoon crushed ginger

1 teaspoon lime juice

2 teaspoons honey

Tools

pot

cutting board

chef's knife

skillet

measuring cups/spoons

spoon

1. Cook the rice noo[dles] package direction[s]

2. Chop the garlic a[nd] pieces and set aside.

3. Heat oil in a skillet over medium-high heat. Add the onion and garlic. Stir frequently to avoid burning. Cook for about two minutes, or until the onions start to soften.

4. Add the broccoli slaw, coconut aminos, ginger, lime juice, and honey. Stir well. The sauce should begin to thicken.

5. Cook for about three minutes before adding the cooked rice noodles.

6. Stir frequently to avoid sticking.

7. Serve immediately.

CHEF'S TIP

This recipe is a wonderful side for the Sesame Beef Skewers.

Allergens Eradicated!

No major food allergens found here!

CHEESY POPCORN

Ready to pop up a snack for movie night? You can impress guests with this cheesy, soy-free popcorn!

Prep Time: 5 minutes

Cook Time: 30 minutes

Makes about 10 cups

Ingredients

¼ cup popping corn

3 tablespoons olive oil

½ cup finely grated Parmesan cheese

Tools

large pot with lid

measuring cups/spoons

roasting pan

spoon

Allergen Alert!

If you're avoiding dairy, nix the Parmesan and go for 2 tablespoons of nutritional yeast instead.

1. Preheat oven to 250°F.

2. In a large pot, place the popping corn and 1 tablespoon olive oil. Cover with a lid and set the burner to medium. Wait until the corn begins popping, and then remove from heat after a minute to avoid burning. Wait until you no longer hear popping, then remove the lid.

3. Pour the popcorn into the roasting pan. Drizzle with olive oil and Parmesan cheese. Stir with a spoon to make sure everything is coated.

4. Bake in the oven for 20 minutes, stirring after 10 minutes. The popcorn should be crispy and coated with cheese.

CHEF'S TIP

Store leftovers in small zip-top bags for tasty snacks to grab on the go.

FRUIT LEATHERS

Reading the ingredient list of processed food can be overwhelming. There are dozens of ingredients, and most of them are too difficult to even pronounce! With only two ingredients, these fruit leathers are nutritious, delicious, and soy-free!

Prep Time: 5 minutes

Cook Time: 6 hours

Makes 24 servings

Ingredients

3 cups your favorite fruit

2 teaspoons honey

Tools

large baking sheet

parchment paper

measuring cups/spoons

blender

spatula

pizza cutter

Allergens Eradicated!

No major food allergens found here!

1. Preheat oven to 150°F. Line a sheet with parchment paper and set aside.

2. If your fruit contains pits, stones, or stems, remove them. Add fruit and honey to the blender. Blend on high until smooth.

3. Spread the blended mix evenly on the lined baking sheet and place in the oven.

4. Bake for six hours, or until the mixture no longer feels wet.

5. Remove from oven and let cool. Carefully peel the fruit leather away from the parchment paper. Use the pizza cutter to cut the fruit leather into strips. Place the strips on parchment paper or roll them up as they are.

6. Place in an airtight container for up to two weeks.

CHEF'S TIP

Need some fruit ideas? Strawberries, blueberries, peaches, pineapple, raspberries, grapes, or bananas work great in this recipe!

CHIPS AND DILL DIP

Skip the soy and make your own crispy, crunchy chips in the oven. Sink your chips into a smooth and creamy dip with a dill-flavored kick.

Prep Time: 10 minutes

Cook Time: 20 minutes

Serves 4

Ingredients

Chips

1 large Russet potato

3 tablespoons olive oil

1 teaspoon salt

Dill Dip

4 stems fresh dill

1 avocado

¼ cup coconut cream

2 tablespoons lemon juice

1 teaspoon dehydrated onion

½ teaspoon salt

Tools

large baking sheet

parchment paper

cutting board

chef's knife

pastry brush

spatula

paper towels

mixing bowl

fork

Allergen Alert!

Coconut is classified as a fruit. But if you have a tree nut allergy, please talk to your doctor before eating it.

1. Preheat oven to 400°F. Line a baking sheet with parchment paper and set aside.

2. Carefully slice the potatoes about $\frac{1}{8}$-inch (0.3-cm) thick or as thinly as you can.

3. Evenly space them on the baking sheet. Make sure the pieces do not touch each other.

4. Brush both sides of each slice with olive oil. Then sprinkle with salt.

5. Place in oven and bake for 20 minutes or until golden brown.

6. Transfer chips to paper towels to absorb extra oil. Allow to cool before serving.

7. For the dip, pull the leaves off of the dill and chop into small pieces. Add to a mixing bowl.

8. Remove the skin and pit of the avocado and scoop the pulp into the mixing bowl. Mash with a fork.

9. Add the coconut cream, lemon juice, dehydrated onion, and salt to the bowl. Stir until smooth.

10. Serve immediately with chips.

11. Store leftovers in an airtight container in the refrigerator for up to three days.

CHOCOLATE DRIZZLE
RICE TREATS

Ready for dessert? Crispy and sweet, these rice treats can be a delectable finish to a soy-free meal.

Prep Time: 10 minutes

Cook Time: 1 hour (1 hour inactive)

Makes 24 squares

Ingredients

½ cup honey

½ cup sunflower butter

1 tablespoon butter

4 cups puffed rice cereal

Chocolate Drizzle

½ cup semi-sweet chocolate chips

1 teaspoon coconut oil

Tools

2 small saucepans

measuring cups/spoons

large mixing bowl

spatula

9 x 13-inch (23 x 33-cm) baking dish

fork

chef's knife

1. Combine honey, sun[...] butter in a small sau[...] heat. Allow the butte[...] until runny.

2. Add the rice cereal to [...] Pour the honey mixture in, stirring with a spatula to coat the cereal well.

3. Using the spatula, press the mixture into a baking dish and allow to cool.

4. While the rice cereal treats cool, make the drizzle. In a saucepan, combine the chocolate chips with the coconut oil over low heat. Stir frequently to avoid burning.

5. When the chips are melted, drizzle the chocolate over the treats with a fork.

6. Allow to cool completely and cut into 24 squares with the chef's knife.

7. Keep leftovers covered at room temperature for up to a week.

Allergen Alert!

Check the labels and contact the manufacturers of your rice cereal and chocolate chips to make sure they are free of allergens you are avoiding.

If you're avoiding dairy, make sure to use a butter substitute instead of regular butter.

Coconut is classified as a fruit. But if you have a tree nut allergy, please talk to your doctor before eating it.

PEACH AND BLUEBERRY
CRUMBLE

Let's get ready to crumble! Dual fruity flavors will tantalize your taste buds with this soy-free dessert. The crumbly topping provides a crunch but also melts in your mouth.

Prep Time: 15 minutes

Cook Time: 45 minutes

Serves 8

Ingredients

4 ripe peaches, fresh or frozen

2 cups blueberries, fresh or frozen

2 tablespoons lemon juice

2 tablespoons arrowroot powder

½ teaspoon ground cinnamon

½ cup rice flour

½ cup packed dark brown sugar

¼ cup oats

¼ cup cold butter

Tools

cutting board

chef's knife

2 mixing bowls

measuring cups/spoons

spatula

8 x 8-inch (20 x 20-cm) baking dish

1. Preheat oven to 375°F.

2. Remove the pits from the peaches and cut into ¼-inch (0.6-cm) slices. Place in mixing bowl.

3. Add blueberries, lemon juice, arrowroot powder, and cinnamon to the bowl and stir.

4. Pour the fruit into the bottom of a baking dish. Set aside.

5. In a second mixing bowl, combine the rice flour, brown sugar, and oats. Set aside.

6. Cut the butter into tiny pieces and add to the bowl, then stir.

7. Sprinkle the topping over the peaches and blueberries.

8. Bake for about 45 minutes, or until the top is golden brown.

9. Cut into 8 pieces and serve warm.

CHEF'S TIP

If it isn't peach season, don't be afraid of frozen peaches. Frozen fruits and vegetables are picked at the peak of their season and frozen immediately. This keeps the freshness and nutrition packed inside. Just let them thaw, and then drain the liquid before you add them to your dish.

GLOSSARY

assemble—to put all the parts of something together

consume—to eat or drink something

discard—to throw something away because it is not needed

drizzle—to let a substance fall in small drops

mash—to smash a soft food into a lumpy mixture

pit—the single central seed or stone of certain fruits

pulp—the soft juicy or fleshy part of a fruit or vegetable

slice—to cut into thin pieces with a knife

thaw—to bring frozen food to room temperature

whisk—to stir a mixture rapidly until it's smooth

READ MORE

Ainsworth, Mark. *The Young Chef: Recipes for Kids Who Love to Cook.* Boston: Houghton Mifflin Harcourt, 2016.

Clark, Pamela. *Allergy-free Cooking for Kids.* New York: Sterling Epicure, 2014.

Cook, Deanna. *Cooking Class: 57 Fun Recipies Kids Will Love to Make (and Eat!).* North Adams, MA: Storey Publishing, 2015.

INTERNET SITES

Use FactHound to find Internet sites related to this book. All of the sites on FactHound have been researched by our staff.

Here's all you do:

Visit *www.facthound.com*

Type in this code: 9781491480564